In the Garden of the Bridehouse

Camino del Sol
A Latina and Latino Literary Series

In the Garden of the Bridehouse

J. Michael Martinez

THE UNIVERSITY OF
ARIZONA PRESS

TUCSON

The University of Arizona Press
www.uapress.arizona.edu

Printed in the United States of America
19   18   17   16   15   14   6   5   4   3   2   1

Cover design by Leigh McDonald
Cover art: *Branched siamese/Siamese ramificato* by Nunzio Paci. Courtesy Officine dell'Immagine, Milan (IT).

Publication of this book is made possible in part by the proceeds of a permanent endowment created with the assistance of a Challenge Grant from the National Endowment for the Humanities, a federal agency.

Library of Congress Cataloging-in-Publication Data
Martinez, J. Michael, 1978–
  [Poems. Selections]
  In the garden of the bridehouse / J. Michael Martinez.
     pages cm. — (Camino del Sol: A Latina and Latino Literary series)
  Summary: "A collection of original poetry in three parts"—Provided by publisher.
  ISBN 978-0-8165-3089-2 (paper : alk. paper)
  I. Title.
  PS3613.A78644A6 2014
  811'.6—dc23
                                        2013047275

♾ This paper meets the requirements of ANSI/NISO Z39.48-1992 (Permanence of Paper).

Strangers to the world, runaways, we are held in the fragile arms of foreignness, each one in the arms of the other's . . .

—HÈLÉNE CIXOUS, *Rootprints*

I am thou, and thou art I; and wheresoever thou mayest be I am there. In all am I scattered, and whencesoever thou wiliest, thou gatherest Me; and gathering Me, thou gatherest Thyself.

—cited by EPIPHANIUS, from the Gospel of Eve

Contents

Acknowledgments

I would like to thank *Crab Orchard Review*, *Eleven Eleven*, *Mandorla*, *Octopus Magazine*, *Phoebe*, *Poetry*, *Quarterly West*, *Rooms Outlast Us*, *Shadowbox Magazine*, and *Spring Gun Press* for publishing early versions of these poems.

Great thanks to Kirk Adkisson, Aaron Angelo, Francisco Aragon, Jennifer Atkinson, Eric Baus, Brian Brodeur, Sommer Browning, Julie Carr, Jules Cohen, Eduardo Corral, Erin Costello, Cynthia Cruz, Lacy Cunningham, Carolina Ebeid, Noah Eli Gordon, Chris Haynes, Paul Kemp, Sara Renee Marshall, Derrick Mund, Eric Pankey, Mark Rockswold, Andrea Rexilius, Carmen Gimenez Smith, Roberto Tejada, Matthew Thomas, Susan Tichy, Vincent Toro and Grisel Acosta, Joshua Marie Wilkinson, Erin and Jordan Windholz, and Peggy Yocom for their friendship and support.

I am particularly grateful for the friendship and editorial advice of Joe Hall and Mathias Svalina.

I would also like to thank the Vermont Studio Center and the Ragdale Foundation for offering such generous time and space for creative contemplation.

Many blessings to Kristen Buckles and the University of Arizona Press for their generosity and support.

In the Garden of the Bridehouse

The Bridehouse says: ——.
touch our names. Seed-
    pods spill silver

hair, leaves, bristle cone,
a caw caught in the belly
of a starved sky. Within our
question, She will say,

In our *you* birth enters;
    in paling ivy,
we are what lovers die.

THE TREATISE OF SWANS

A Collection of Transposed Portraits

Self-Portrait as the Soul Excluded, My Speechless

words were a species   of bell between childhoods

    a menagerie of copper   wire

        lodestar
        & the feminine

wild   before the vulnerability

    of precious things

sang me toward the birdless ruins

Self-Portrait as One-Night Stand

Your brutal empty
pull plum-

        bruises
perfectly men perfect

I apple my Adam pale
                I shiver me doll
      a paper darkness
                   twining

to die   & pass—the fountain
to my   *in you* is our

self to   solitude
ward you   looking for me

Self-Portrait When We Were New Animals Across an Ancient Sky

Exquisite in our throat
a hallowed wet opens.

Our limbs melt.   Our creature's fat

is this given rawness of things.
If we could but carve

our signature
in swine, in saltpeter, in sperm-
less amen

the moral would cease   as the fable's interruption.

Knitting decisions we submit
to our savage:

where light opens internal
to light itself,   my pleasures of you

write laws within ribbons
of honey hanging

from suet.   Sickle-sweet,
our body begets every place suitable

for prayer
& lips.

Self-Portrait as the Hinge Within the Fable

Imagine—in front of us—they silently pass. And they believe unrelated
        objects are organs
to recognize the human. And, again, we are no longer interruptions.

Imagine—in front of us—the beginning is not a study. And they believe
        the cicada's larva
reveals narrow secrets. And we accompany: to form, to shape.

Imagine—in front of us—a beautiful garden. And they believe color is
        the shoreline's end
where we abandon our too sudden bodies. And, here, we are carriers
        of different significance.

Imagine—in front of us—each word devolves a lexicon. And they believe
        shape shuts on a hinge
within the voice they fable. And, here, we slaughter the spring lambs.

Imagine—in front of us—they pass us between nature, between history.
        And they believe the door
alters the frame's flow. And we are a dark summer moving against oceans.

Imagine starlings circling in a postcard's blue. And they believe oration is
        the living thing, the end
of geometric space. And here, in full sunlight, we are gifts hoisted to the vanishing point.

Self-Portrait as Your Voice, Trying to Stop an Echo

wherever tidal water

foams salt-
water flowers

against stone

darker we echo

wed to a death

grown young
our tears

learn of radiance

outside gravity   —   wholly present tense   —   we suffer

the angels in the children
our bodies were

Self-Portrait as the Polaroid of You

This withdrawal of color into form,
kittens & creamer,

all the soft
preventing my own
absolute individual—

To name the water
after you—when I die,
I want the young languages

to paint the pier
with the vigor & goodness
of the devout,

to distinguish two points
between judgment
& perception:

our thoughts in what they represent,
& our head bound by the background.

Self-Portrait as the Record Player's Needle

I carved a record out of frozen Irish creamer. I wanted it to sound like coffee poured through silk. At the limits of reason, I sought to seduce you. But you wanted me to stop buying happiness: blue dog dolls, banker lamps, and puddles for birds. You wanted me to run with you through worm-laden forests & shed black petals. But there is no movement between the object & my body, only these certainties: a match, a lamp, a self withdrawing into its appearance.

Self-Portrait as Letter Addressed to Self

. . . . . ,

Someday, across glacier, a green horse will ride toward you; despite steam rising from heavy breath, you'll touch its snout.

When you paired a person's gait to signature, what lilt signed your step? What tautology was this body's hypothesis?

Do you remember your mother's *Strawberry Fruit-Salad Recipe*? 2 round angel cakes (2 pounds or 4 halves), 16 oz. of vanilla pudding, 4 bananas, 2 containers of 8 oz. strawberries, 1 big container of whipped cream. Layer and eat.

Your hands shaking, you wrote, "Christ is sentiment."

A cup cracked through with sky. A saucer planed into the shapes of numbers. Every written thing stripped bare, the more supple formulation of given law.

I told you distance to a thing is the purchase of its reality. Why are people like that for us? The more we love the more physical space our love inhabits & the world's lightnesses & darknesses assume the order of human tongue.

Last night we tore & tossed memories into ponds. Geese swam across, pecked the waters. I splashed at them &, after, my hands shook. You stood beside me in a red dress. I wanted to drown you this pretty.

xoxo,
. . . .

Self-Portrait Where We Sing of Such Wounded Swans

Two-inch porcelain swans
unfold egg-

shell thin feathers

as scars,
& small

meteors spit

up from wheels of red
carriages we ride when felled

apples no longer
bruise
into brown halos.   We smile

out of a window

of stamps, cherry stems
tongue-tied around   such promise of *yes*.

Self-Portrait as a Grim Tale
The King Who Took His Daughter to the Boiling

But before the daughter was the day an army of loyal servants wearing only silk slippers spread out in a hundred rows across a thousand acres of flora. The animals fled these naked & their soft plodding. Poppies, wisteria, calla lilies were razed from earth & hung from pins onto sheets of vellum. The librarians organized the plants according to their alchemical properties—motherwort, lady's mantle, & mistletoe paged together under the heading of "Life Root." The books of flora were taken to the cauldron's depth to the cauldron's culler. The albino culler opened the books of the flowers, dipped the thousand stems & petals, calyxes & bulbs into a molt of gold.

After the lily's fall & the wisteria's orbital ridges were shelled in amber, the king rushed from his throne with salivating hands. He took one of the culler's arrangements to his garden, planted it delicately in moist dirt. He climbed to his topmost tower. Purple robes fell over his crooked arms. He trumpeted orders from a conch shell. Wearing black cotton garments & leather boots, the servants spread out in obedience across the fields, replanting what had been torn.

But before the daughter & before the flora was the day the king ordered three stones a day to be taken from his keep. Stone on stone for a thousand days of stone until all were pliable sublimations of light. White apron against albino face, the culler bowed. The king, seated on his throne, stood before his supplicants. He climbed to the highest mounds of golden blocks. Purple robes fell over his crooked arms. He trumpeted orders from a conch shell. Dressed in white cotton garments & barefoot, the servants, standing in one hundred & one rows, bowed simultaneously & set to the task of rebuilding. On the throne the king sat light-bowered, his frame a mineral embodied & alive.

In the Garden of the Bridehouse

The Bridehouse says: ———. The Bridehouse says:
The sun's center is the child
before everything
agreed to the grammatical
gender. Before Law
dipped its salt tablet
into blood, & mouth
became elegy, She said,
tributaries may return
water to formless air,
choirs may unfold acacia
within mortality, & we will wear
more allegory than flesh.

Self-Portrait When We Were Animals Called Ocean, Called Honky, Called Baby

We burden one
                    we birth in none

body coiled beneath water
            body lawless in expression

to singularize
        we
            name-carve the distant

At birth, they drowned on embryonic fluid, body bypassing the point between birth & breath. After resuscitation, they were isolated in a white room. Needles crowned the skull, waters breathed before breath filtered from pockets puffy beneath the skin. When released, they were diagnosed with a "surface condition." Kept to the interior of living rooms, bedrooms, & basements, they learned to crawl beneath coffee tables, amid groves of chair legs. Once, their mother took them to the shade of a maple, blankets sheltering them in the stroller. A warm breeze tickled leaves into clucking tongues. Their father played baseball. After, their mother glimpsed through the covering. Their exposed fingers, faces were traced in veins, blistering. Their brother roared as a lion on the lawn. At dusk they joined the world's spare-light. The year later they dressed in Sunday suit: blue vest, pants, blue tie. Their parents walked them to a playground. As she watched them crawl beneath a swing, their Tía teased, "Whose honky baby is that?" Ashblack slapped against skin.

The first man   we loved shackled

                    our
penis in hand   thumbnail tip-
pinching mirror's   face the first woman

we loved   suckled our tongue
tongue   swallowing

        mirror down to moan's trespass

The sixteenth-century cobbler & German mystic Jacob Boehme practiced his craft in his home of Gorlitz, the easternmost town in present-day Germany. Imagine, exhausted, Boehme, face thin & long, reads the heretical texts of Paracelsus by candlelight. He checks his Bible against the alchemist's conjectures. He falls to sleep in such posture. The following morning, Boehme goes outside & comes across a pewter bowl. As he picks up the dish, the dawn rises over the horizon, & light breaks against the pewter's curve.

We cut our hand   @ straddles our tongue

@ we echo for *eidos*
with feet between intention

& Being

we consequence   callused with promise

flowers opposed to edict

Startled, Boehme charts in shattered light the spiritual architecture of creation. Concerning the creation of the manifest universe, his depictions are an unsettling phantasmagoria of humanity's advance out of/into grace. One illustration depicts Boehme's Adam before Adam's will turns to lust for the material world. The illustration's geometrical mapping of the soul demonstrates less the Edenic origin of humankind than how language operates at the gravitational center in one cobbler's vision of paradise. Adam is not a human body, corporeal, gendered. At the diagram's center, a star burns amid divine fire. Adam is *within* & *of* a sphere pregnant with the synthesized alchemical symbols of water & air, the integrated feminine & masculine: @.

We other hunger   the flower whose roots succor

        changeless intimacies

the *un* of communion shaped from deeper root

        our betrothal

    in wreathes of polished bone

        we become dioramas
        we become & die

        or am I

        the pulses' monsoon

My diluvium Eve

animal we are
we are too

many skies

flesh we listen
flesh we black one

ribcage buries
what holy

becomes medallion

Creation we corrupt
with precedence

what other story could
grow children

Micrographia

or Some Physiological Descriptions of Minute Bodies Born in the Garden of the Bridehouse

He is Lord and Lady of duality
He is Lord and Lady of our maintenance
He is mother and father of the gods, the old god
He is the god of fire, who dwells in the navel of fire
He is the mirror of day and night
He is the star which illumines all things,
and he is the Lady of the shining skirt of stars
He is our mother, our father
He is Ometéotl who dwells
in the place of duality, Omeyocan

—Translated from Nahuatl by MIGUEL LEÓN-PORTILLA,
Aztec Thought and Culture

/jénisis/

[Ancient Greek γένεσις origin, creation, generation, the root of γίγνεσθαι to come into being, be born; the same Indo-European base as classical Latin *gignere* to beget: see genital *adj.* + -σις-sis *suffix*.]

i. In Hebrew, the book is called *Bĕrēʾšīṯ*, literally 'in the beginning', after its opening words.
ii. The action of building up from simple or basic elements to more complex ones; opposed to *analysis*. Cf. synthesis *n*.
    a. †*Math.* The process of obtaining a given power of a number.

—OED

A generation after origin,   the wild grass opened
into body.   I-blind, *Bĕrēʾšīṯ* voiced flesh to beget
eyeless compasses, mouthfuls of hummingbirds,
the choir we became   to oppose concord.
Dawn   enclosed   our   lips   in   solar   light.
We   sang   letters,   what   was   animal
vanishing   into   umbilical   throes.

The Gospel of Ometéotl, the Brown Adam

People walk through you, the wind steals your voice / you're hurra, huey, scapegoat, /
forerunner of a new race / half and half—both woman and man, neither— / a new gender
—GLORIA ANZALDUA, Borderlands/La Frontera: The New Mestiza

Jasmine garlands thin
   for the rib's cartilage ring.

The heart shudders with pure mission.

        She spreads
        & knows herself as Adam,
        Ometéotl,

        but through himself,
        Omecíhuatl,

        he is Eve.

   He knows but what the garden gives:

     the garden's soot
     awakened tongueless in root.

Cerise chrysantha
   coils around his leg.

Gathering the tides
      of the seas to his side,
      she conceives

      where impossibilities seed.
Clarity burning coal, he takes two knots

                              of grass
                            & strings

              four birds of paradise
        through the ceiba's rotted leaves:

                        she fashions the sorrows
                        from winter's purse,

                        sea
                        & sun

                        sifted for sum.

              Intrammeled, Ometéotl rises
                        one among one

              body stitched in strange altar.

In the Garden of the Bridehouse

The Bridehouse says: ———. The Bridehouse says:
beneath the bridal wreath. Suffer a man
before a table spread with laughter, he bears
history as singular music, or he relives
childhood in the hunger of bees
sucking the blonde stems
of a woman in her question
& asparagus crawls the tree
as branches blaze carmine shoots.
Suffer the woman in the man
& we are a cell in which I have lived:
a square room cut into the earth, a ladder leading
to the light above, blindness seeking our eyes,
images the felt flesh, words
our fingers begging for the lips.

The Chrestomathies of Omecíhuatl, Giver of Life

Appendix to the Gospel of the Brown Adam

Is my birth a reason, a corporeity bound to guilt?

> *Our body is the nave*
> *lathed from the ceiba,*
>
> *from fragmented unities.*

King David raped the south wind / bathing in the brook / laid in spice.
He tore / Bathsheba's breasts with lips, / their fragrant reed / sung. The
pomegranate trees / flared bronze, the woman's eyes, / doves strapped
to a seat of purple wool.

> *Re-*
> *cover betray*
>
> *al of your seed, the "I,"*
>
> > *hands made*
> > *of bitter wax.*

How? When?

Remember, while you sleep, I will touch your lips to possess no tongue's shape; rather, seas sealed beneath splintered ice, the generation & name.

> *In the year after, I will write: —/ hollowed within eyes /*
> *In the year after, you will write: —/ of tears & blood clots /*

/iːv/

[Fem. proper name, from Biblical first woman, Late Latin, from Hebrew *Cha-wah*: living being, to breathe; Middle English *Heve* even *n.*; for the loss of the final *-n* see maid *n.1*; repr. *yeve*, the regular (now obsolete) southern form of *give v.* In midl. dialects *give* is used in same sense.]

   i.   The name = evening *n.1 lit.* & *fig. poet.* or *rhetorical.*
   ii.   *Transf.* The time immediately preceding some event, action, etc. Chiefly in phrase *to be on* or *upon the eve of.*
   iii.   *Intr.* To become moist or damp.

—OED

Where all suddenness awakes to homecoming,
she glories as a shrine in a glade
of crescent reeds. The noun breeds
a beast of silk.
She wrings writing of mirrors & harvests the beetles
in their bed of letters. Naked of body,
she grinds a paste to plant a wilderness
between penance & pleasure,
flowers of feral syllables.

Omecíhuatl in the Garden Where *Yes* Is the Only Island

(from the *Gospel of the Brown Adam*)

Is anything stable and lasting? What reaches its aim?
        —*Cantares Mexicanos*, folio 10, v.

Untenable surface swarmed

in light, water-striders,

& mauve strings
of sea moss pattern

grammar   in the thin wind's swill.
I tear water

from our chest. Swept in thorn,
                our lips stained

        with agarita, I feed
        the chalice-vine, succoring

our nature   before we are organs.

                        If this
—the grey-green leaf, the gift-led blind—
        is deity, our language is soaked

in the black's brine.   The black sings

        a music nudity banners,

        a field of scorched arms
        of what was once

acres of pine.   Soothing soot

                        across our face,
                        we sing

over flowering world.
Separated, we are. Why

      this field of racked hunger

when the lion's mane
once carried the calendars? No longer

over life but of life,
we burn the resin surviving

the eye.   We build

altars from breath's broken splinters.
        I count your breath,

remember our skin   as *the silence making*

    silence real, a garden

        where *Yes* is the only island.

The Chrestomathies of Omecíhuatl, Giver of Life

Appendix to the *Gospel of Ometéotl, the Brown Adam*

When lovers gaze through water & know the shape of duration, why does my
imperfection press between my shoulder blades as a stare?

The pen-

> *etrating eye*
> *casts the hour's*

shadow. Form
& identity

> > > *shatter desire*
> > *to presence: dunes*
> > *with winds shaping broken*

> > > *figures out of sand.*

Spring buds chill in early April frost. When I press my finger into the world
beneath the grass, why am I Other in Winter's ash?

> *Beneath the clavicle's narrow,*
> *we loam & rake*

> *tumors to language self of shadow.*

> *In love, we live laced*
> > *in Other voice,*

> > *hem*
> > *& seam.*

You told me to pour water until the aster overflows. Soil spilled onto the floor. I cannot keep. I can't will this lovely grid, the compass hollow where my belly splinters.

Meager, incarcerate dawns will us

    as hand to hammer
    our gesture:

a forge whose tongs translate scarlet joys

    out of blood,
    out of poppy.

    Of each other,

    we speak bodies whole.

/ˈædəm/

[Hebrew *ā-dām* man, earth.]

i.   The name given in the Bible to the first man; hence *fig.* as in the phrase *Old Adam*, the 'old man' of St. Paul (*Rom.* vi. 6, etc.): the unregenerate condition or character.

ii.   Phr. *not to know* (a person) *from Adam*: not to recognize him; *(as) old as Adam*: primevally old.

—OED

I unwrapped the light from origin's aviary,
wing   &   beak   sewed
through an apron of leaves.   I pinned her
against a hymn.   I bit her lip to pulse
our organ   &   thresh   desire   for   salt.
For the heart's other hunger, the skin in wondrous
agony,   I   said,   he   gazed   the   sound.
I meant she split the plot. He said, I, I said her
letters   fell   from   my   dress   of   flesh,
every edge an erosion unsheathed from speech.

In Dominion, the Breath's Hammer

(The Botanical's Confession of Distinction)

Bowed beneath bloated limbs,
the Name grew

   like anemone: a colt cantered
     before her
snorting steam;

   taking a handful of sand,
   she fed the animal

   its passage from dust.

She said,
   my pet, my grace—tear us pale,
   perish my lungs so wingless.

                 ᕱ

On grasses beneath, the man

& woman
were each other. The woman

   took the man's head
   in her hands, parting   his scalp into a gulf;

    a carob tree grew from the opening;

   his brown hair coiled coral vine
     through the branches.

     He caressed her neck,
     eased his hand in

     until her trachea was
     sheathed in palm.

Coiled in boughs—He said, When grace is exhaled, life is time without negation,
        our bodies bridged across dust-weighted air. Said, Consign the tongue
        to the hesitance between hammer & peal, the body will awake deathless,
        clothed in acacia.

Against the tree, She said, Inscribed between leaves light-sharpened, trumpet-
        shaped, a raw human forest resigns between tongue & tooth. The man
        took her hair, wound it into braid.

❧

From stem
      & branch I saw

the animals approach.

        White moth,
     magenta-flecked wing incandescent,

sea urchin, broad-tailed hummingbird,

      wasp wing herded by wren song & lion breath
        down rows of juniper smoke:

      with wooden hook & blade
man & woman peeled   the animal's skin from scalp,

        the bay, the caw

        of lamb
        & crow

        cut
      from tongue, bound to myrtle—

   the pelt, the hind

                become alphabet.
Deprived of signature,

      the animals stood in the ark's descent,
      all that was without language.

The serpent curled
          from umbilical stem,

she cradled me in palm,
where incandescence ascribes definition,

sweet blossoms drifting deathless into authorities. The man took her palm,
          with a blade cut her finger base to nail, said, This to approximate a world.

                                        He then bit to my white:
                                        his body opened as an eye.

               I lay on the grass where dropped:

                                        a worm curled in me, eating,
          whispering to seed   as they blossomed to flesh.

The Chrestomathies of Omecíhuatl, Giver of Life

Appendix to the *Gospel of the Brown Adam*

I have tasted womb & shaft, my body bore their tides. Why do our lips mortar against grace & confession? Within us, how does name-giving birth the hour the hours open?

We named water   to your body

        where our bodies were

          opened. You tasted

                    the wound's salt,

             the nape of the pure

        mouth hungering

                the tremor across the opalescent.

Death enters between language & autonomy—my love, darkness sings

             water unto

                unto water.

But you said, no water veils, no narrative wrapping the flower.

I say, Sharpen the knives against stone's heart, gut its guilt.
Measure the length the shell of our body.

But would you return me?

I would return winter's fall from frost, the organ from pulse,
Love, your death praises wholeness on our altar, its door unlocking our human space.

Where Timid Gestures Black

(Eden's "I" mmigrant)

I unsettle speak
                    & swift

my pale tint
argue   what white

                    ೕ

            is passport
            water-speckled spic

            they nation   *territory into tradition*

            an aerie zone, a

                    ೕ

            space they two-faced
            & abbreviated the eggs

                    of our garden

                                before
                                God
                                nested & layed

                    beaks of an English-

                    ೕ

    wish speaks within
                my Adam

                    with such violence

                    weeds sprung

from our palms   love turned
                   into the

we refuse to bear   I am

            ❧

      a man as

                                    a woman within
                                    a question posed

      afterimage
      exposed through
      physical fact
      & psychic effort

            ❧

we weave   such celluloid
walls my wet-
      back Eve   & such love

      spic spacs my Adam

         a light inside

      where timid gestures black
      the aperture be-

            ❧

tween where we
      are most strangers

         we are
      our fear lodging

            ❧

         the distance

                                    of intimacy
                                    from the lie
                                    solitude is

      language again

The Chrestomathies of Omecíhuatl, Giver of Life

Appendix to the *Gospel of the Brown Adam*

It is said that the little children who died, like jade, turquoise, and jewels, do not go to the frightful and cold region of the dead, *Mictlan*. They go to the house of *Tonacatecuhtli*; they live by the "tree of our flesh." They nourish themselves on the tree of our sustenance....

— CHICHIHUACUAUHCO, as described in *The Florentine Codex*

I have tasted the expired breath, the wish made oxygen.
Why this place lost between branches? How cast the near-life?

Our body collapses for birth, for interbelonging. In life, we are metaphor's open belly: proper dwelling of nous, thumos, & epithumia. In passing, this fullness of possession becomes, not immolation, but immanence.

But held as a speechlessness, my body is flayed into ribbons. A multitude of silences gather me in their beaks & twine me through entrails. A cuckoo lays her egg in the nest I've become. I peel the shell & see my laughing head cradled in sombrero.

Metaphor for the @: uncertain death, always anterior to the dialectic between Self as Subject & Self as Object. At birth, the @'s womb penetrates metaphor as time, a gift by which the heart's gaze is purified, tormented by the world in the worlds revealed through us.

I journey to the other side of the image in the mirror: a black lock of hair, a burial chamber, grimacing teeth, a child's cry held in a vase.

I stand by my mother's coffin, counting the rosary beads in her clasped hand. The rosary beads count the number of lips locked in prayer, the prayers count her worlds unarrived.

Who but us to sorrow the tree, its aver to leaf

In the Garden of the Bridehouse

The Bridehouse says: ———. The Bridehouse says:
the dying wing. Enter the space of the cry.
Define the hand the cry
questions, or the child's
beseeching before the mother
is the father mourning the ash rot,
counting small pearls
of flesh left on the petal after slaughter;
or is the woman walking the path
toward syllable's end?
Infant's name withheld until infant is able
to sieve the sun's bridal wreath?

THE CHILD'S DREAM OF ASTERS

In order for music to free itself, it will have
to pass over to the other side . . . where the
structures collapse . . . where a powerful song of
the earth is unleashed, the great ritornello that
transmutes all the airs it carries away and makes
return.

—GILLES DELEUZE, *Essays Critical and Clinical*

The Child's Dream of Asters & the Water's Elegy

The Folk Tale of La Llorona: A Cantata in Three Voices

When the Spanish arrived in Mexico, they were impressed by the beauty of the Indian children. The Spanish took the children (the most beautiful) and gave them to their wives. Some of the Indian women drowned their children in order to keep the Spaniards from taking them. *La Llorona* is one such woman. She now is searching constantly for her children, whose faces she sees in all children. She kills the children to be united with her own again.

—Bess Lomax Hawes

The Child (Soprano)   ....nonitalicized text
The River (Baritone)   ....italicized text
The Mother (Tenor)   ....with score

Accompanied by the score broken below a child's dark heaven

before, I wake: the aster's   after, I dream: the amber

petals spread   your hand the wax comb

across the surface   mold I crush as my body

a human-shaped pollen   swarms into scattered

wings gathering the milk.

Waking & shushed, I smile

    & home:

    coarse swathe
    of black wool, pig

    heads on pikes,
    a basket of *chapolines*, your sigh

    lathes you
    to my ear.

You parted my body
in narrow bands

Waking, I clasp

> your callused hand,
> your hair's braided coal,

> my fate of sky.

Tumors bud on the river branch. Pearling holly. Bruising plum.

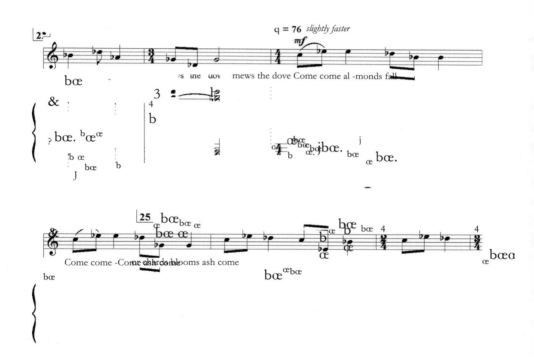

lit -tle child Coo -coo Coo coo Shade to ringing to death

Watching	You grind the corn
I follow	You gather the bits
Watching	You boil the water
I follow	You roll the masa
Watching	You pray the beads
I follow	You worship the guilt
Watching	You shape to husk
I follow	You cut the meat
Watching	You strain the blood
I follow	You soak in spice
Watching	You keep the fire
I follow	You stir for light
Watching	You cup the ash
I follow	You suck the lime
Watching	You heat the iron
I follow	You swaddle me warm
Watching	You take me for kiss
I follow	You tender my cheek
Watching	You ash my locks
I follow	You feed me song
Watching	You swallow me singing
I follow	You grace the furrow
Watching	You, I come to water
I follow	You, I song my life

Hand in hand the river we sing

                        strung to-

                        gether

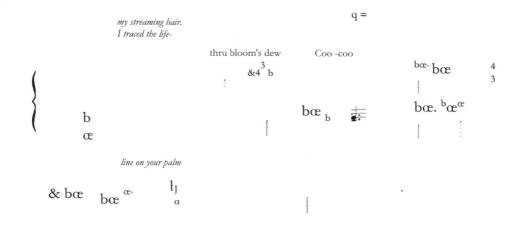

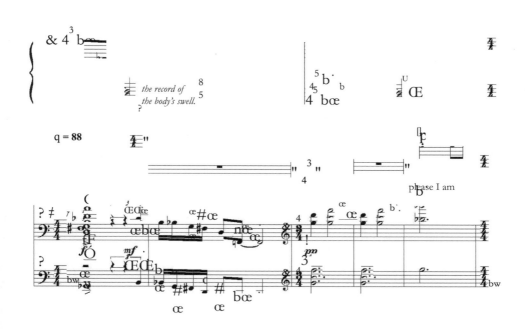

Through the water's   veil, the water streams
                            & cracks

your thousand faces   into a single

        skin fresh under my nails,

brings you close to me. I touch
                the black ravines without tree,

the black birds whose hollow bones already flute music.

[75] [Mother]

Coo coo Coo -coo -mews the dove Coo

[81]

The river washes   your throat :: tumors open
                          to petals :: of attestation

The river wishes   the head against head :: gap veiled in the meadow
                          sounds no longer :: asters burnt & curdled as milk

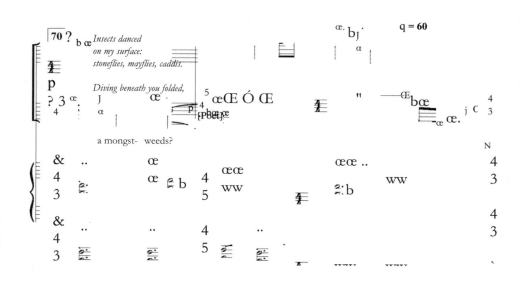

[70] Insects danced
on my surface:
stoneflies, mayflies, caddis.

Diving beneath you folded,

a mongst- weeds?

q = 60

57

contracted, contorted
until movement broke,
exhausted of breath

The river spills

the depths of torpor :: the black lamb's wool
ribcage opened :: rib lung-cored

The river spells

as if there are no words :: black rock moving against
brush :: love in no space hemmed

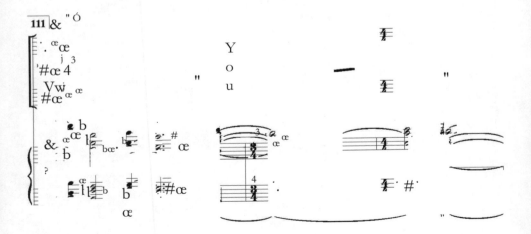

You watch	I grind the water
You watch	You gather the bits
You watch	I boil the current
You watch	You roll the beads
You watch	I pray no song
You watch	You worship the guilt
You watch	I shape to husk
You watch	You cut the life
You watch	I strain no blood
You watch	You soak in spice
You watch	I keep the fire
You watch	You stir for light
You watch	I cup the ash
You watch	You swaddle me warm
You watch	You tender my cheek
You watch	You feed me the song
You watch	You swallow me singing

strung to-
gether

strong to
gather

The river spills   bittersweet I :: pollen for flesh
                     bittersweet I :: hive for song

the river spells
of my thigh, your love
like sand, like stone
hair tangling upward

your linen's wet :: white-wash
    water wilt :: willow leaf's
            laughter :: clotting

You must go, they will find you...

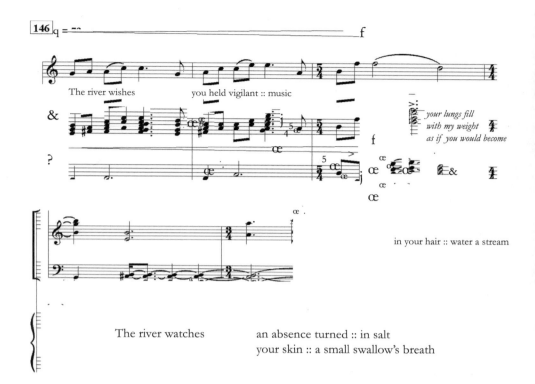

The river wishes   you held vigilant :: music

your lungs fill
with my weight
as if you would become

in your hair :: water a stream

The river watches   an absence turned :: in salt
                           your skin :: a small swallow's breath

I wake the aster I dream

                amber petals spread your hand

                                                              the water-life

                the wax comb across the surface   *the surface light*

                                                              makes known.

                mold crushed as my body

                a human-shaped pollen swarms

                into scattered

                            wings

le music here. {

In the Garden of the Bridehouse

The Bridehouse says: ———. The Bridehouse says:
language then flesh, flesh then allegory.
If resurrection, the coiled flame authoring
the heat of every felt form,
would you remember the pollen-
heavy pregnancy
of lisianthus before the scream
inside our stars
fell through
the botanical? Skin sea-
moss soft, the Eden my tears
remember . . . I held you
death in hands when our hands
were branded with the letters
radiance pulls
through the scab
of name's touch.

The Bridehouse's Harmonograph

$$x(t) = x1(t)+x2(t),$$
$$y(t) = Ay(t)\sin(wyt+py)$$

$$x2(t) = As(t)\sin(wst+ps)$$

A = amplitude of oscillation in our image, our likeness

w = frequency of false weights, false measures

p = the phase between nudity & the palace of perfect dawns

s = the rotational factor wherein memory reconciles with redemption

$$x1(t) = Ax(t)\sin(wxt+px)$$

The music's portrait

where plurality marries for singularity
the Bridehouse is

into nudities
& dawn palaces
between exiles &

the strangers aboard me   build ruins again.   as ocher leaves   refuse to sing
        Spring equations   their map   rings the octave

❧

Apples no longer

❧

Notes

In the Garden of the Bridehouse

&

By allowing the "butterflies of song" to be born in himself, the Nahuatl wise man began to express "that which is true on earth." And the painter, "the artist of the black and the red"; the sculptor, carver of the signs that measured time and of the images of gods and myths; all of the philosophers, musicians, architects, and astronomers sought the same thing—their own truth and that of the universe. Nahuatl philosophic thought thus revolved around about an aesthetic conception of the universe and life, for art "made things divine," and only the divine was true. To know the truth was to understand the hidden meaning of things through "flower and song," a power emanating from the deified heart.

—Miguel León-Portilla, *Aztec Thought and Culture*

Self-Portrait as Your Voice, Trying to Stop an Echo
the vulnerability of precious things From Simone Weil, *Gravity and Grace.*

The Gospel of Ometéotl, the Brown Adam
Miguel León-Portilla, in his *Aztec Thought and Culture*, describes the deity Ometéotl. Ometéotl, in its manifestations, as the Lord and Lady of duality, is both feminine and masculine at once. In its feminine manifestation, Omecíhuatl, the Lord and Lady extend out into the various other deities of the Mexica pantheon. León-Portilla describes Ometéotl as inhabiting the garden Omeyocan, the land of duality. Ometéotl is duality as singularity, the two that is one (2:1). He also describes Ometéotl as appearing from a lake of glass as a creature of a single torso, male and female incomplete and intertwined. His words describe the deity as bouncing around "like a sparrow" and in an infinite embrace.

The Chrestomathies of Omecíhuatl, Giver of Life
In *The End of the Poem*, Giorgio Agamben writes, "For Augustine, this experience of an unknown word (*verbum ignotum*) in the no-man's-land between sound and signification is the experience of love as will to know."

Omecíhuatl in the Garden Where Yes Is the Only Island
the silence making silence real From Thomas Merton, *Thoughts on Silence.*

Where Timid Gestures Black

territory into tradition From Homi Bhabha, *The Location of Culture.*

The Child's Dream of Asters and the Water's Elegy

The folk tale of La Llorona is a classic Chican@ narrative. As told, La Llorona is an indigenous mother who drowns her children after being spurned by a Spanish lover. She returns as a banshee, drowning children who wander too close to the river.

The Bridehouse's Harmonograph

The harmonograph is a nineteenth-century instrument used to draw the numerical value of musical tones on an X/Y axis. An octave, with the numerical value of 1:2, appears like butterfly wings. Here, the harmonograph, using numerology representing Ometéotl, is an octave. The shape is filled out by the present manuscript's language, cut and pasted hundreds of times.

About the Author

J. Michael Martinez received the Academy of American Poet's Walt Whitman Award for his book *Heredities*. He is a PhD candidate at the University of Colorado, Boulder.